Air

by Henry Pluckrose

Gareth Stevens Publishing
A WORLD ALMANAC EDUCATION GROUP COMPANY

Please visit our web site at: www.garethstevens.com
For a free color catalog describing Gareth Stevens' list of high-quality books
and multimedia programs, call 1-800-542-2595 (USA) or 1-800-461-9120 (Canada).
Gareth Stevens Publishing's Fax: (414) 332-3567.

Library of Congress Cataloging-in-Publication Data

Pluckrose, Henry Arthur.
    Air / by Henry Pluckrose. — North American ed.
        p. cm. — (Let's explore)
    Includes bibliographical references and index.
    ISBN 0-8368-2957-3 (lib. bdg.)
    1. Air—Juvenile literature. 2. Atmosphere—Juvenile literature.
    [1. Air. 2. Atmosphere.] I. Title.
    QC161.2.P57   2001
    551.51—dc21   2001031111

This North American edition first published in 2001 by
Gareth Stevens Publishing
A World Almanac Education Group Company
330 West Olive Street, Suite 100
Milwaukee, WI 53212 USA

This U.S. edition © 2001 by Gareth Stevens, Inc. Original edition © 2000 by Franklin Watts.
First published in 2000 by Franklin Watts, 96 Leonard Street, London, EC2A 4XD, United
Kingdom. Additional end matter © 2001 by Gareth Stevens, Inc.

Series editor: Louise John
Series designer: Jason Anscomb
Gareth Stevens editor: Monica Rausch
Gareth Stevens designer: Katherine A. Kroll

Picture credits: The Stock Market – cover, p. 9 (T. & D. McCarthy); Tony Stone Images pp. 6
(Darryl Torckler), 10 (Eddie Soloway); Images Colour Library pp. 19, 28, and title page; James
Davis Travel Photography p. 12; Still Pictures pp. 27 (Thomas D. Mangelsen), 31 (Thomas
Raupach); Robert Harding pp. 15 (Jon Gardey), 20 (Schuster/Dr. Müller), 23 (David Hughes),
24 (Schuster); Image Bank p. 17 (A. T. Willett); Impact p. 4 (Francesca Yorke).

Printed in the United States of America

1 2 3 4 5 6 7 8 9 05 04 03 02 01

Contents

Air around You 4

A Mixture of Gases 6

Breathing 8

Wind 10

Wind Direction 12

Flying Kites 14

Hurricanes and Tornadoes 16

Using the Wind 18

Using Air. 20

Hovercraft. 22

Warm and Cool Air 24

Flight 26

Traveling through the Air. 28

Polluted Air. 30

Index / More Books to Read 32

Although you cannot see air, air is everywhere. Wherever you are, whether you are awake or asleep, air is all around you.

Air is a mixture of different gases. This mixture of gases surrounds Earth like a blanket. A gas is something that is not a liquid or a solid.

All living organisms, such as plants and animals, need air. When you breathe in, you take air into your lungs. Air contains a gas called oxygen. Your lungs take oxygen out of the air. You need oxygen to survive.

When air moves, we call it wind. On a windy day, we can feel air moving all around us.

Although we cannot see air, when the wind blows, we can see the direction in which air is moving.

It is fun to fly a kite when the wind blows. The moving air holds the kite up and makes the kite twist and turn.

The winds of tornadoes and hurricanes are powerful and move very fast. These winds are so strong that they often damage objects in their paths.

We also can use the power of the wind to make machines work. Wind moves the arms, or blades, on a windmill. The moving blades turn gears inside the windmill. The gears operate a machine that may grind grain, pump water, or even produce electricity.

Air is used in many different ways. Maybe you have worn armbands filled with air to help you float in water. The tires on these bicycles are also filled with air. Do you know why?

A hovercraft is a type of vehicle that floats on air. Fans on the craft blow out air beneath it, making a cushion of air on which the craft can move over land or water.

Air expands, or spreads apart, when it becomes warmer. Warm air is lighter than cool air. The air in this balloon is heated by a special burner, so the air inside the balloon becomes warmer and lighter than the cooler air around it. The warm air rises, lifting the balloon off the ground.

Birds fly through the air. Their bodies are shaped to let air move easily around them. The shape of their wings is especially important. Air moving above and below their wings helps them fly.

Some cars and trains are shaped so they can move smoothly through air. The shape of this train helps it move through air very fast. It is called a "bullet train." Do you know why?

Clean air is very important for many reasons. We need to breathe clean air to stay healthy. Smoke from cars, trucks, and factories can make the air dirty, or polluted. We must all try to keep the air clean.

Index

armbands 21

bicycles 21

birds 26

breathing 8, 30

Earth 7

electricity 18

floating 21, 22

gases 7, 8

hot air balloons 25

hovercraft 22

hurricanes 16

kites 14

lungs 8

oxygen 8

smoke 30

tornadoes 16

trains 29

wind 11, 13, 14, 16, 18

windmills 18

wings 26

More Books to Read

Experiment with Air. Experiment With (series).
   Bryan Murphy (Lerner Publications)

Feel the Wind. Let's Read and Find Out Science (series).
   Arthur Dorros (Ty Crowell)

Hurricanes. Natural Disasters (series).
   Victor Gentle and Janet Perry (Gareth Stevens)